SURVIVING BETRAYAL

Albert 'Femi Oduwole
A publication of Triumphant Publishing House (TPH)
Published by: Triumphant Publishing House
G.P.O. Box 16245, Ibadan, Nigeria.
www.albertoduwole.com

ISBN: 978-978-978-246-8

All rights reserved. No part of this publication may be reproduced, stored in a retrieval system or be transmitted in any form or by any means; mechanical, electronic, photocopying or otherwise without prior written consent of the copyright owner.

1st edition

NOVEMBER 2020

Dedication

This book is dedicated to the survivors of betrayal. Keep shining, you are the real MVP. YOU ARE TRIUMPHANT.

Acknowledgements

I am grateful for the gift of men. I have always believed that my 'main gift' is not speaking, writing or leading. My main gift however, is 'the gift of men.' Thanks to: my nuclear family, siblings, in-laws, spiritual sons and daughters (especially those who encouraged me to write this book and work on it with me), mentors, protégées, and colleagues.

I really am GRATEFUL!

Introduction

'BETRAY'. The word is an eighth of an inch above 'betroth' in the dictionary, but a world from betroth in life. It's a weapon found only in the hands of the one you love. Your enemy has no such tool, for only a friend can betray. Betrayal is mutiny. It's a violation of trust, always an inside job." - *Max Lucado*

Here is a must-read because the question is not 'will I ever be betrayed'? For that is sure, but 'am I equipped to survive betrayal'? Nobody is immune from betrayal, it is either you have been betrayed or you are being betrayed or you will be betrayed. There's no way you won't fall into any of these categories.

This book gives insights into the following and more:
- Understanding betrayal
- Why betrayal hurts
- Why people betray
- Surviving betrayal
- What to do if you are the one that betrayed

THE LAMENTATIONS OF THE BETRAYED – KING DAVID JESSE

12.   'This isn't the neighborhood bully mocking me-I could take that. This isn't a foreign devil spitting invective-I could tune that out.

13.   It's you! We grew up together! You! My best friend!

14.   Those long hours of leisure as we walked arm in arm, God a third party to our conversation.

15.   Haul my betrayers off alive to hell—let them experience the horror, let them feel every desolate detail of a damned life.

16.   I call to God; God will help me.

17.   At dusk, dawn, and noon I sigh deep sighs—he hears, he rescues.

18.   My life is well and whole, secure in the middle of danger even while thousands are lined up against me.

19.   God hears it all, and from his judge's bench puts them in their place. But, set in their ways, they won't change; they pay him no mind.

20.   And this, my best friend, betrayed his best friends; his life betrayed his word.

21.   All my life I've been charmed by his speech, never dreaming he'd turn on me. His words, which were music to my ears, turned to daggers in my heart.

22.   Pile your troubles on God's shoulders - he'll carry your load, he'll help you out. He'll never let good people topple into ruin.

23.   But you, God, will throw the others into a muddy bog, cut the lifespan of assassins and traitors in half. And I trust in you.'

Psalms 55:12-23.

Table of Contents

Chapter One

UNDERSTANDING BETRAYAL

"Is it possible to succeed without any act of betrayal?"- Jean Renoir.

/be·tray·al b   trā l, bē trā l/ noun. Betrayal is the action of betraying one's country, a group, or a person; treachery. Synonyms: disloyalty, treachery, bad faith, faithlessness, falseness, duplicity, deception, double-dealing; breach of faith, breach of trust, stab in the back; double-cross, sell-out; perfidy.

Betrayal in relationships. Betrayal in workplace. Betrayal in family. Betrayal in ministry. There are tales of acts of betrayal strewn all over. And its stings hurt many years after it has taken place. Betrayal is as old as the earth. And many wonder of its increase in recent times.

There has been quite a lot of discussion about the end-times especially since the advent of COVID-19. The Bible in no way shrouds its occurrence. Rather, it actually gave us multiple signs of the end-times and a major one of such is BETRAYAL. It will be in such great measures that the love and trust of many will wax cold.

'And then many will be offended, will betray one another, and will hate one another.' Matthew 24:10. NKJV.
'Then many false prophets will rise up and deceive many.' Matthew 24:11.
'And because lawlessness will abound, the love of many will grow cold.' Matthew 24:12.

In fact, Jesus describes it as "betrayal unto death," the worst kind. 'Now brother will betray brother to death...' Mark 13:12. NKJV. There are different shades of betrayal. It can come from multiple sources and in varying degrees. In this book, I want to zero in on five different types.

FIVE TYPES OF BETRAYAL
1.   SELF
"Of all betrayals, self-betrayal is the worst and the most difficult to forgive" Anonymous.

Sometimes, we sin against ourselves. We falter and make grave mistakes that are in contrast to what is true to our convictions of what is right and acceptable. At this point, we often feel we have not been true to our innermost self. We feel we have betrayed ourselves and it hurts terribly to forgive ourselves for not living true to what we feel is godly or ethical.

Yes! It is sometimes more difficult to forgive the culprit if that culprit is 'you'. Have you discovered that it is much more difficult to forgive oneself than it is to forgive others? It is called 'guilt'; and that is not of God but of the devil.

Forgiveness makes the future possible. Remember that you cannot get ahead by getting even. Let yesterday go! If you've been out of a healthy relationship with God and fallen out of order, repent of the deed. Ask for forgiveness. God can be trusted to forgive you.

'Come now, and let us reason together, says the Lord. Though your sins are like scarlet, they shall be as white as snow; though they are red like crimson, they shall be like wool.' Isaiah 1:8. The Amplified.

'If we confess our sins, he is faithful and just and will forgive us our sins and purify us from all unrighteousness.' 1 John 1:9. New International Version.
God did not only promise to forgive. He says it in a superlative form. He assures that He will 'abundantly pardon.' (Isaiah 55:7). In other words, He will lavishly forgive you. He will pardon you graciously. Your transgressions will be wiped off your screen like it never popped up in the first place. Glory to God!

It's time to move on. Do not listen to what the devil is saying about your past. Satan is rightly addressed as the 'accuser of the brethren.' He discusses your past. That appears to be the only information he has. On the other hand, Jesus discusses your future, Alleluia!

Coming into relationship with Jesus transforms your life. When He comes in, He puts an end to the past and gives birth to a new tomorrow. Turning to Christ will move you from hindsight to foresight. The truth is; you cannot help where you have been, but you can help where you are going.

John Rice said, "No matter how terrible your past is, your future is spotless." There's need to move on. You need to understand that 'what lies ahead of us is greater than what lies behind us. Yet, what lies within us, is greater than them all.' Move on towards God, not away from Him. For when He sees a breach, He will build a bridge and when He sees a scar, He will make a star.

Forget about your present position. For even when you are down to nothing, God is still up to something. Forget about your opposition, for when you mind opposition, you might lose your position. Forget about your embarrassment, for those that have embarrassed you in the past will soon embrace you.

Today is your day of salvation. You must therefore move on. As the saying goes: 'Yesterday is a cancelled cheque, tomorrow is a promissory note, today is the only cash you have, so spend it wisely.'

Move on! Success is the sweetest revenge against yesterday's hurts and pains. LET YESTERDAY GO!
Don't call to heart the mistake of yesteryears. Yesterday will hold your future bound for as long as you let it. You must forge ahead and pick yourself from the dirt. Forgive your frailty in falling short. You must let go of your flaws and press into something fresh that is awaiting you in your future. Tomorrow is untainted, embrace it.

2.   FAMILY

"Now brother will betray brother to death, and a father his child; and children will rise up against parents and cause them to be put to death." Mark 13:12. (NKJV).

Another very terrible betrayal is the one that occurs within the family. To be betrayed by friends is bad enough but to be betrayed by family is very terrible. The popular saying 'blood is thicker than water' is enough to calm one's nerves in relating with family members. It should be the norm for our family members to love us and support us as we 'do' life. Quite incredibly, betrayal is sometimes strong enough to break through the thickness of blood. I have seen many die of heart attack, high blood pressure and several diseases after being swindled in business, betrayed within close-knit family relationships and so much by close family members. The pain sometimes is not just about what is done but who did it!

3.   FRIENDS

'God, defend me from my friends, from my enemies I can defend myself.' African Proverb.

Friends, whether in writing or pronunciation ends with "...ends". I like saying 'your friends will determine your end.' It could be a very bitter end when betrayal is involved.

This is how David expressed such:
"It's you! We grew up together! You! My best friend! We took sweet counsel together, and walked unto the house of God in company." Psalms 55:13. (The Message).
14 'We used to share our secrets with one another, as we walked through the crowds together in God's Temple.' Psalms 55:14. (ERV).

20 'And this, my best friend, betrayed his best friends; his life betrayed his word.
21 All my life I've been charmed by his speech, never dreaming he'd turn on me. His words, which were music to my ears, turned to daggers in my heart.'
Psalms 55:20-21. The Message.

4.   MARITAL

"All partners of abuse will always carry the scars and a deep sense of loss and grief from the betrayal. Those that stayed, left, or been left, it must be remembered that time is the salve on this journey towards forgiveness and healing, because there is also a process of grieving." - Meryn G. Callander.

Marital betrayal is brutal. It destroys trust which is the backbone of marriage. Like I always say "Love is a gift, but trust must be earned."

Love, forgiveness and trust are three important words in human relationships. As close as they are, they are so different. If I rode a horse and it threw me off, I can easily forgive because I love the horse, but before I ride it another time I will be more careful. I have forgiven but trust is another issue. Forgiveness can come in an instant, but it takes time for trust to be built.
Trust cannot be demanded, it can only be earned with a lifestyle of truth, for truth builds trust. Distrust results in destruction of many marital relationships and it will sure take time and truth to build trust.

Heartache is the result of marital betrayal. The main problem with heartaches from heartbreaks is that there's no hospital where it is treated. The medical world has specialists for everything, but to the best of my knowledge, there is none yet for heartbreaks. When it occurs, we have to go back to the Maker.
'He heals the broken-hearted and binds up their wounds.' Psalms 147:3 (NKJV).
The Passion Translation (TPT) assures that even if the heart is shattered, it is healable by the Maker of hearts. 'He heals the wounds of every shattered heart.'

## 5.	ORGANIZED

"Organized betrayal is the bane of destinies, for it destroys many. Many that betrayed. Many that are betrayed and many that could have been blessed."

Organized rebellion is rebellion against authority. The devil was the first to organize a successful coup d'état. Since then, and up till now, organized rebellion has destroyed several organizations (both spiritual and secular alike). From organizations, congregations and nations, organized rebellion has left behind disastrous stories everywhere.

Organized betrayal is 'mutiny'. It is always 'a scheme to topple or remove constituted authority', and according to the quotes above, it affects more than the betrayed and the betrayers, but countless others that could have been blessed from the stable organizations, congregations and nations.

Chapter Two

<u>WORST BETRAYAL STORIES</u>

THERE ARE DIVERSE stories of betrayal in the history of man. Each of these holds a peculiar twist to how the trusted became the traitor. There are different versions to each of them. Of all these, there are some that are outstanding. They could rightly be termed 'Worst Betrayal Stories'.

I.   THE BETRAYAL OF JESUS

Matthew 26 tells the story of how Jesus was betrayed. Verses 14-16 let us in on how Judas Iscariot went unto the chief priests to bargain with them on betraying the Master to them for a token. The agreement was mutually agreed upon, and in verse 16, the bible says 'And from that time he sought opportunity to betray him.' NIV. He executed his intention in verse 49.

Jesus was sold out with a kiss by one of His disciples. Judas was no ordinary disciple; he was entrusted with the purse. He was the only one with a position; and not just any position but that of a treasurer.
Reading the account of the story from The Message Translation drives home certain salient truths.

46   'Get up! Let's get going! My betrayer is here.
47   The words were barely out of his mouth when Judas (the one from the Twelve) showed up, and with him a gang from the high priests and religious leaders brandishing swords and clubs.
48   The betrayer had worked out a sign with them: "The one I kiss, that's the one- seize him."
49   He went straight to Jesus, greeted him, "How are you, Rabbi?" and kissed him.
50   Jesus said, "Friend, why this charade?" Then they came on him- grabbed him and roughed him up.'
        Matthew 26:46-50. The Message.

I want you to note very carefully that 'the slap of a friend is better than the kiss of a betrayer'. Furthermore, it is not every show of affection that is sincere. Some are traps of destruction. You must be watchful.

2.   BENEDICT ARNOLD

Benedict Arnold was a brave Revolutionary War General before he became a traitor. In Saratoga, N.Y., there is a strange monument. It comprised the sculpture of a boot and the inscription of praise that fails to mention (by name) the one being memorialized.

That monument is in honour of Benedict Arnold, a brave Revolutionary War General before he became a traitor. His actions helped in avoiding disaster at the battle of Saratoga. When Arnold tried to sell out West Point Colonial Fort, he became a traitor. He later commanded a redcoat army against the colonists. At a later date, he went to England, where a few praised him, but most reviled him. He was given land in Canada, but that did not help him find any security or comfort in his latter days.

Someone thought Arnold deserve some kind recognition for his early bravery; but because he was anathema, his name never was mentioned on the inscription. His boot however was memorialized because he had been wounded in the leg in battle.

The life of Arnold holds a deep lesson. It shows something about traitors. Their memory is always bittersweet. It is sweet for the period of belonging but bitter for the moment of betrayal. Whatever good they might have done is obscured by their act of betrayal.

3.   MARCUS JUNIUS BRUTUS

"Et tu, Brute?" - William Shakespeare, Julius Caesar.
No treachery is worse than betrayal by a family member or friend. Julius Caesar knew such treachery. Among the conspirators who assassinated the Roman leader on March 15, 44 BC was Marcus Junius Brutus. Caesar not only trusted Brutus, he had favoured him as a son.

According to Roman historians, Caesar first resisted the onslaught of the assassins. But when he saw Brutus among them with his dagger drawn, Caesar ceased to struggle and, pulling the top part of his robe over his face, asked the famous question, "You too, Brutus?" And subjected himself to the deadly wound of the assassins.

4.   SAMSON – THE BETRAYAL OF A WARRIOR

The Book of Judges (from Chapters 13 to 16) recounts the betrayal and fall of a warrior. Samson, (Hebrew Shimshon) was a legendary Israelite warrior and judge. He was renowned for the prodigious strength that he derived from his uncut hair.

Samson's incredible exploits (as related in the biblical narrative) hint at the weight of Philistine pressure on Israel during much of Israel's early, tribal period in Canaan (1200 -1000 BCE). The biblical narrative, only alluding to Samson's "twenty years" activity as a judge, presents a few episodes, principally concerned with the beginning and the end of his activity.

Before his conception, his mother, (a peasant of the tribe of Dan at Zorah, near Jerusalem) was visited by an angel who told her that her son was to be a lifelong Nazarite (one dedicated to the special service of God, usually through a vow of abstinence from strong drink, from shaving or cutting the hair, and from contact with a dead body).

Samson possessed extraordinary physical strength. The moral of his saga relates the disastrous loss of his power to his violation of the Nazirite vow, to which he was bound by his mother's promise to the angel. He first broke his religious obligation by feasting with a woman from the neighbouring town of Timnah, who was also a Philistine (one of Israel's mortal enemies). As a mighty man, other remarkable deeds characterised Samson's life.

For example, Samson decimated the Philistines in a private war. On another occasion he repulsed their assault on him at Gaza, where he had gone to visit a harlot. He finally fell as a victim to his foes through loving Delilah, who beguiled him into revealing the secret of his strength (his long Nazirite hair). As he slept, Delilah had his hair cut and betrayed him. He was captured, blinded, and enslaved by the Philistines.

At the end, God granted Samson a comeback through the return of his old strength. He demolished the great Philistine temple of the god Dagon at Gaza where he destroyed his captors alongside himself.

On a light mode, this is probably the most expensive haircut in the world. According to the bible story, she was promised 1100 pieces of silver by each of the philistine rulers who approached her to betray Samson. The bible did not indicate the number of rulers there were, so there's no way to calculate the sum. Pondering on the story of Samson, it is good to glean one truth. Be careful whose lap your head is placed on because you might end up losing it.

5.   THE BROTHERS OF JOSEPH

Joseph the son of Israel (Jacob) and Rachel lived in the land of Canaan with eleven brothers and one sister. He was Rachel's firstborn and Israel's eleventh son. Of all the sons, Joseph was loved by his father as his favourite. To that end, Israel arrayed Joseph with a "long coat of many colours."
Israel's favouritism toward Joseph caused his half-brothers to hate and betray him. When Joseph was seventeen years old he had two dreams that made his brothers plot his demise. In the first dream, Joseph and his brothers gathered bundles of grain. Then, all of the grain bundles that had been prepared by the brothers gathered around His bundle and bowed down to it.

In the second dream, the sun (father), the moon (mother) and eleven stars (brothers) bowed down to Joseph himself. When he told these two dreams to his brothers, they despised him for the implications that the family would be bowing down to him sometimes in the future. They became jealous that their father would even ponder over Joseph's words concerning these dreams. (Genesis 37:1-11).
They saw their chance to execute their plans when they were feeding the flocks. The brothers saw Joseph from afar and plotted to kill him. They turned on him and stripped him of the coat his father made for him. After this, the brothers threw him into a pit.

As they pondered on what to do with Joseph further, they saw a camel caravan of the Ishmaelites coming out of Gilead carrying spices and perfumes to Egypt, for trade. Judah (the strongest) thought twice about killing Joseph and proposed that he be sold. The traders paid twenty pieces of silver for Joseph and the brothers took Joseph's coat back to their father. He was lied to and informed that Joseph had been killed by wild animals.

Sibling rivalry and betrayal is very common. Parents should avoid showing favouritism among their children. It breeds hate. The coat of many colours can easily become the coat of many sorrows when dipped into the blood of treachery and betrayal.

Chapter Three

WHY BETRAYAL HURTS

"The worst pain in the world goes beyond the physical. Even further beyond any other emotional pain one can feel. It is the betrayal of a friend." Heather Brewer - Ninth Grade Slays.

In the bible passage earlier quoted; Psalms 55:14-23, King David explains to us why betrayal hurts. If you have been betrayed before, I am sure you will find some resonance with his feelings and lamentations as recorded in that bible passage.

1.   IT'S COMMITTED BY A FRIEND

"To betray you must first belong." - Harold Philby.

The saddest thing about betrayal is that it is an offense only a friend can commit. That is because in order to be betrayal there must have been trust first. And according to King David, that is why it hurts! The memory of wounds by friends brings pain.

20   'And this, my best friend, betrayed his best friends; his life betrayed his word.

21   All my life I've been charmed by his speech, never dreaming he'd turn on me. His words, which were music to my ears, turned to daggers in my heart.'

Psalms 55:20-21.

2. IT MAKES YOU FEEL STUPID AND DOUBT YOURSELF

"It was a mistake," you said. But the cruel thing was, it felt like the mistake was mine, for trusting you." David Levithan (The Lover's Dictionary).

Betrayal leads to self-doubt. You will keep wondering on why you have been so 'seemingly' stupid enough to have trusted and failed to discern the disloyalty.

Perhaps you've heard the story about the little swallow. It was covering one eye with its wing and crying bitterly. An owl flew by and asked, "Little bird, what's wrong?" The swallow pulled away its wing and showed a gash where once it had an eye. "Now I understand," hooted the owl, blinking, "You're crying because the crow pecked out your eye!" "No," replied the bird sadly, "I'm not crying because the crow pecked out my eye; I'm crying because I let him."

You are likely to have forgotten that hindsight is always perfect and that people wiser, greater and more spiritual than you have also experienced betrayal at one point or the other. The best you can do is to turn back to the all-knowing God (in prayers) for deliverance and peace.

16   'As for me, I will call upon God; and the LORD shall save me.

17   Evening, and morning, and at noon, will I pray, and cry aloud: and he shall hear my voice.

18   He hath delivered my soul in peace from the battle that was against me: for there were many with me.'
Psalms 55:16-18.

3.   IT SHATTERS DREAMS

"I am not crying because of who you are because you are not worth it, but I am crying because of the illusion of who I thought you are." Anonymous.

Every act of betrayal shatters dreams. Dreams of what could have been through the union and relationship. Rather than God changing His mind He will rather change the man. The fear is not in the dream not coming to pass, but the fact that mostly we have dreamt it with someone or some people.

It hurts! David said in Psalms 55:14 'We took sweet counsel together and walked unto the house of God in company.' The ERV says of that verse 'We used to share our secrets with one another, as we walked through the crowds together in God's temple.'

4.   IT ALWAYS LEAVES A WOUND AND THEN A SCAR

"For there to be betrayal, there would have to have been trust first." Suzanne Collins - The Hunger Games.

The wound of betrayal is not in not forgiving the culprit(s), but the inability to trust again. If you don't properly heal from those that betrayed you; you will bleed on those who believe in you.

No wonder David the king prayed and cried day and night for total healing. It is only God who can heal the pain, wound and scars of betrayal.
Confidence in an unfaithful man in time of trouble is like a broken tooth, and a foot out of joint. Proverbs 25:19.

5.   IF CARE IS NOT TAKEN, IT DESTROYS YOU

"Everyone suffers at least one bad betrayal in their lifetime. It's what unites us. The trick is not to let it destroy your trust in others when that happens. Don't let them take that from you." Sherrilyn Kenyon - Invincible.

Do not let betrayal destroy you. It has destroyed many marital dreams, political ambitions, etc. Betrayal can either leave you bitter or better. The choice is yours. Even if betrayal has devastated your past or present, it must not be allowed to destroy your future. It's time to draw the line between a betrayed past and a better future.

22   Cast thy burden upon the Lord, and he shall sustain thee: he shall never suffer the righteous to be moved.

23   But thou, O God, shalt bring them down into the pit of destruction: bloody and deceitful men shall not live out half their days; but I will trust in thee.
        Psalms 55:22-23.

Chapter Four

<u>WHY PEOPLE BETRAY</u>

ALTHOUGH THERE IS no justification on why people should engage in betrayal, there are countless reasons people indulge in this act. Many people find it hard to accept the fact that they betrayed and it ought not to be. They are quick to point out why.

WHY PEOPLE BETRAY
1.   PERSONALITY
"Sometimes it's not that the people change, just that the mask fell off."

There are some people that are just in themselves predisposed to a lifestyle of betrayal. Their antecedents show it. I once had a man betray me by taking over a branch of our organization. In retrospect, it occurred to me I should have been more sensitive. He has always toppled all his superiors everywhere he had belonged.

Solomon the wise warned us against such people.
'My son, [reverently] fear the Lord and the king, and do not associate with those who are given to change [of allegiance, and are revolutionary].' Proverbs 24:21. The Amplified.

From his dual position as the king and the preacher, Solomon had encountered so much betrayal and he was able to warn us about the characters of those who betray.

He said 'be careful of them'. They always:
1.	Spread mean gossips
2.	Start fights
3.	Stab in the back

He invariably described traitors as calloused climbers ready to stab people's backs to get ahead. They wouldn't mind that of their very own friends and even grandmothers.
What a shame!

27	'Mean people spread mean gossip; their words smart and burn.
28	Troublemakers start fights; gossips break up friendships.
29	Calloused climbers betray their very own friends; they'd stab their own grandmothers in the back.
	Proverbs 16:27-29. The Message.

## 2.	UPBRINGING
Everyone is a product of two things:
1.	Nature
2.	Nurture.
Nature is how we are wired but nurture is activated by training and environment. It is sad that some people by their upbringing are schooled in the very art of betrayal.
Sometimes, the environment you were nurtured in sharpens you to excel in certain endeavours. For instance, growing up in a polygamous home with all its dramas is like going to school for a master's degree in betrayal.

Also; it is sad to note that, in many cases of betrayal between spouses, one or both (sometimes engage) their young children as partners. They include them in the betrayal of trust and the marital vows; thereby nurturing the kids in the very act of betrayal.

I met a lady who had a very wrong disposition to infidelity. She feels it is not out of place to have extramarital affairs while keeping it as a secret from one's spouse. She saw it as being normal and acceptable because she grew up seeing her mother do same.

This also plays out in corporate organizations. Some are unfortunate to have a mentor that King Solomon described above as 'callous climbers'.
Such character traits become the norm for them. They have no iota of guilt because they are actually living by their upbringing!

It is always important for us to learn as parents. We must not withhold the 'rod'. We can (through our godly lifestyles and discipline) root out betrayal traits early enough in our children. An example is seen in the case of David and his rebellious son; Adonijah. The Bible says David never disciplined him once.

5   'At about that time, David's son Adonijah (his mother was Haggith) decided to crown himself king in place of his aged father. So he hired chariots and drivers and recruited fifty men to run down the streets before him as royal footmen.

6   Now his father, King David, had never disciplined him at any time – not so much as by a single scolding! He was a very handsome man and was Absalom's younger brother.'
1 Kings 1:5-6. The Living Bible.

This seems to be a weakness for King David because we can see the same pattern with him raising his first son (Amnon) after he betrayed his step-sister by raping and disgracing her.
 21 'King David heard about this, he became very angry. But David didn't punish his son Amnon. He favoured Amnon because he was his firstborn son.'
2 Samuel 13:21.

Stop finding reasons for indulging the traits of betrayal in your children. David indulged Amnon because he was his firstborn (the very reason why he should have trained him better). He indulged Adonijah because he was handsome. What is your reason for indulging betrayal? He is hardworking, or she is rich etc. None of these is acceptable. No matter how 'reasonable' the reason is, the venom of betrayal is deadly and it won't spare the perpetrators.
The truth is; no matter your reason for indulging betrayal traits, it will always boomerang!

3.   WRONG INFLUENCE
Everyone is a product of influence.
In my about five decades on earth, I have seen loyal people become disloyal because of bad influence. Almost always, betrayal by trustworthy folks is birthed by coming under wrong influence.

The 'influencers' are skillful in the art and science of betrayal. They know how to catch their 'prey' in a vulnerable state and 'corrupt them with flatteries'. I have seen this play out severally in ministries. The influencers come saying things like:
- 'You are a better preacher than our General Overseer'
- 'I enjoy listening to you than listening to papa'
- 'If not for you in this ministry, all of us would have left'

If you are not careful, they will 'make you act against your covenant by corrupting you with flatteries'.

'And such as do wickedly against the covenant shall he corrupt by flatteries: but the people that do know their God shall be strong, and do exploits.' Daniel 11:32.
In many marital betrayal stories, it sometimes starts with 'seductive talks'.

'The king of the north will play up to those who betray the holy covenant, corrupting them even further with his seductive talk, but those who stay courageously loyal to their God will take a strong stand.' Daniel 11:32. The Message.

I love the last part of the verse above.

'Them that will stay courageously loyal ...must take a strong stand.'
 I have had my share of such negative influencers in my marriage and ministry. Thanks be to God, I've got the cure! I learnt it from King Solomon. Here it is:

'The north wind driveth away rain: so doth an angry countenance a backbiting tongue.' Proverbs 25:23.

Yes an ANGRY LOOK. That's the perfect cure.
You need to rehearse such looks in readiness for them. That look stops disloyal gossips, flatteries and their cohorts.

You need to be wary of another set of people. Beware of folks that always repeat to you only the negative things 'others' are saying concerning you. They are sent to dump baggage on you and take information from you to report in other quarters. If they are really

for you and have your true interest at heart, their angry looks should have stopped the negative influencers in their tracks.
I always say to such people:

'Don't tell me what they said about me; tell me why they are comfortable to say those words in your presence?'

That is a very vital question to ponder on for tale bearers. That is because his or her body language must have made such discussions easy for the so-called influencers. It will shock you that some folks like Zacchaeus of old profit by false accusation!

'And Zacchaeus stood, and said unto the Lord; behold, Lord, the half of my goods I give to the poor; and if I have taken anything from any man by false accusation, I restore him fourfold'. Luke 19:8 .

4.   WRONG SPOUSE

I am known in many quarters as a 'MARRYmatician'. That might be because I have a bestselling book on Amazon and other platforms with the title 'MARRYmatics'. It could also be due to the fact that I teach a lot along this topic.

I have realized that if you marry a wrong spouse even the devil will give you a break. Why am I so sure? Satan knows what will destroy you has already moved in with you. To that end, there's no point wasting his meager resources.
I am known for saying this from time to time:

'If you marry right you've got a prayer partner, but if you marry wrong you've got a prayer point.'

If you must run a fruitful and peaceful organization, ministry and family, be sure you give attention to who your 'associates' marry. I will use this scripture to show you an example of biblical proportions:

'But there was none like unto Ahab, which did sell himself to work wickedness in the sight of the Lord, whom Jezebel his wife stirred up.' 1 Kings 21:25.
The Message Translation drives it home in a better form:
'Ahab, pushed by his wife Jezebel and in open defiance of GOD, set an all-time record in making big business of evil'.
 If you got a wrong spouse just like Ahab and Jezebel you can set an all time record of betrayal. What makes this worse is that, most of the time, such mothers produce after their kind (or fathers as the case may be).
 Later a young king from a good family married from the Ahab and Jezebel dynasty. The same situation was repeated. King Jehoram the son of Jehoshaphat followed the same trend.

'And he walked in the way of the kings of Israel, as did the house of Ahab: for the daughter of Ahab was his wife: and he did evil in the sight of the Lord.' 2 Kings 8:18.

For this reason; when any of my associates wants to marry, in as much as we won't dictate, we strongly investigate and advise accordingly!

5.   STUPIDITY

It is surprising to discover the number of people whose disloyalty is a product of utter folly. I have seen people that became disloyal to their spouse, pastor, leader etc. because they lack knowledge. It will shock you how many folks are disloyal out of plain stupidity.

'Two hundred men went with Absalom from Jerusalem. But they had been called together knowing nothing of the plot and made the trip innocently.' 2 Samuel 15:11

Look at The Message Translation
'And with Absalom went two hundred men out of Jerusalem, that were called; and they went in their simplicity, and they knew not anything.'..

Imagine. Two hundred folks followed Absalom without having a clue on why they are acting in that manner. They lack the real reason for following him. They had 'zeal without knowledge'.

Disloyal leaders always prey on easy folks to use as foot soldiers and human shields. Unfortunately, such folks are the ones that suffer more because; to the rebel leader, they are just a pawn to be played for his /her personal interest.

6.   HURTS & OFFENSES

Hurts and offenses is the underlining factor of many betrayal stories. Jesus already predicted and prophesied that in the end time hurts and offenses will increase. To that end, disloyalty will multiply.

'And then shall many be offended, and shall betray one another, and shall hate one another.' Mathew 24:10.

When I counsel many people that are or have been disloyal, the major explanation remains 'If you know what he/she/they did to me/us you will understand why I/we resolved to being disloyal'.

Unfortunately, offenses make you forget two of the great 10 irrefutable laws of relationships (as stated in my book GET INSPIRED - RELATIONSHIPS)

LAW 8
THE LAW OF CORPORATE DESTINY
"The destiny of men are linked, the key to someone's destiny is hidden in the destiny of another."

The key to Elisha's destiny was kept in the destiny of Elijah, that of Saul in Samuel and that of Paul in Barnabas. Men are ladders that are meant to take people to their next level. There are some men you must meet up to move up. They hold the key to your next promotion. The saying is very true: 'you don't need to know everyone, just the right people.' In the same vein that, 'you don't need every key, just the right key to open the door'. There are some relationships you cannot afford to toy with because your destinies are linked.

Be nice to people you meet on your way up because they might be the push you need (to go back up) on your way down. "Never abandon a friend', either yours or your Father's. Then you must need to go to a distant relative for help in time of need." Proverbs 27:10.

LAW 9
THE LAW OF CONFLICT RESOLUTION
"It is better for the situation to be resolved than for the relationship to be dissolved."

Maturity is the ability to disagree and yet hold hands. If indeed our relationships are product of corporate destiny, then we must not allow offences to break it.

Here are tips to handle conflicts:

1.   If you are right, don't rub it in.
2.   If you are wrong, accept it!
3.   Even though offences will come, refuse to be offended. Injustice is only as powerful as your memory of it.
4.   Never be bitter. Betrayal is not as worse as bitterness because betrayal destroys your past but bitterness will destroy your future.
5.   Forgive, because 'forgiveness makes the future possible'.

The Amplified Version of the holy bible did grand justice to the words of Jesus in Mathew 24:10.
'And then many will be offended and repelled and will begin to distrust and desert [Him Whom they ought to trust and obey] and will stumble and fall away and betray one another and pursue one another with hatred.'

 Make sure you heal well from your hurts and offenses. Failure to do so will lead to this:
'If you don't heal well from who cut you, then you will eventually bleed on those who didn't cut you!'

This is a major issue. Many people pay Paul with disloyalty for the offenses of Peter. I have seen this severally in marriage, ministry etc.

7.   DEMONIC INFLUENCE
 Unfortunately there's a lot more to disloyalty. In so many cases, there's a supernatural dimension to the natural scenarios.
'And supper being ended, the devil having now put into the heart of Judas Iscariot, Simon's son, to betray him.' John 13:2.

Do not be deceived, there's more to betrayal than meets the eyes. The betrayal of Jesus, for example had the devil's hands in it (as stated above).

The devil infiltrates his thoughts. There are always three thoughts in the heart of men.

1.   Thoughts that originated from you
2.   Thoughts that originated from God
3.   Thoughts that originated from the devil

The third example is what you have to be careful of. That's why the wise preacher of old, King Solomon says:

'Above all, be careful what you think because your thoughts control your life.' Proverbs 4:23. Easy to Read Version.

Here is the litmus test for godly thoughts according to Apostle Paul.

Philippians 4:8- TPT.

'So keep your thoughts continually fixed on all that is:

-        Authentic and real
-        Honorable and admirable
-        Beautiful and respectful
-        Pure and holy,
-        Merciful and kind.

And fasten your thoughts on every glorious work of God, praising him always'.

So, garrison your heart with pure thoughts to prevent thoughts of betrayal from filtering in. Eventually, they will lead to the act.

8   WORKS OF THE FLESH

Man is designed as a tripartite being. He is a spirit; he has a soul and lives in a body. All through the Holy book, believers are encouraged never to allow the flesh to lead and rule them. In fact the great Apostle Paul said no matter how spiritual you are, there will also be a struggle between being led by your spirit or by your flesh. (Galatians 5:17).

To yield to the flesh is to yield to all the 'ingredients' of betrayal as itemized below:

19   'Now the works of the flesh are manifest, which are these; adultery, fornication, uncleanness, lasciviousness.
20   Idolatry, witchcraft, hatred, variance, emulations, wrath, strife, seditions, heresies.
21   Envyings, murders, drunkenness, revellings, and such like: of the which I tell you before, as I have also told you in time past, that they which do such things shall not inherit the kingdom of God.'

Here is another rendition of Galatians 5:20-21 by The Message Translation:
20   'Trinket gods; magic-show religion; paranoid loneliness; cutthroat competition; all-consuming-yet-never-satisfied wants; a brutal temper; an impotence to love or be loved; divided homes and divided lives; small-minded and lopsided pursuits.
21   The vicious habit of depersonalizing everyone into a rival; uncontrolled and uncontrollable addictions; ugly parodies of community...'

I am sure you can see these look like betrayal. They are 'acts that lead to "divided homes and divided lives"' according to the scriptures above.

The solution to this is also in the scriptures:

'But I say, walk and live [habitually] in the [Holy] Spirit [responsive to and controlled and guided by the Spirit]; then you will certainly not gratify the cravings and desires of the flesh (of human nature without God).' Galatians 5:17. The Amplified.

9.   HARVEST OF BAD SEEDS SOWN

There's a law in the Bible that God promises will last unto the end of the world. It is called the law of SEEDTIME AND HARVEST.

'For as long as earth lasts, planting and harvest, cold and heat, summer and winter, day and night will never stop.' Genesis 8:22. The Message.

This means if you get a harvest, simply check what you have sown. If you want a different outcome, please change your input. See how Jesus explained it as it relates to betrayal:

'Then said Jesus unto him, put up again thy sword into his place: for all they that take the sword shall perish with the sword.' Mathew 26:52.

But Jesus told him, "Put your sword away. Anyone who lives by fighting will die by fighting." CEV.
In other words, most people who succeeded in betraying others end up being destroyed by the betrayal of some others. There are too many examples to prove this is true. David perfectly understood this truth. As a young anointed king, he did not betray Saul to mount the throne. This explains why he refused to kill Saul when he had the 'opportunities' to destroy him. Later, he taught his followers the same. That explained why (later in life) the betrayal attempts of Absalom and others against him never worked out.

8	Abishai said, "This is the moment! God has put your enemy in your grasp. Let me nail him to the ground with his spear. One hit will do it, believe me; I won't need a second!"
9	But David said to Abishai, "Don't you dare hurt him! Who could lay a hand on God's anointed and even think of getting away with it?"
10	He went on, "As God lives, either God will strike him, or his time will come and he'll die in bed, or he'll fall in battle.
11	But God forbid that I should lay a finger on God's anointed..."

1 Samuel 26:8-11.

That's why Solomon (may be out of his experiences advised):

'The one who returns evil for good can expect to be treated the same way for the rest of his life.' Proverbs 17:13. (TPT).

This explains why I believe there is no need for you to curse those who betray you. It's only a matter of time. Many people understand this and will refuse to plant bad seeds of betrayal. They however forget the other side of repaying loyalty with a great harvest. 'An hypocrite is he that fights people for betrayal but refuse to reward loyalty.'

David understands how to reward loyalty. I greatly admire this trait in him. Even when the loyal person was no longer alive, David looked for his descendants to bless them. The wisdom is, 'your loyalty today affects your descendants tomorrow. Be careful.'

'One day David asked, "Is there anyone left of Saul's family? If so, I'd like to show him some kindness in honor of Jonathan." 2 Samuel 9:1. The Message.

ACTS OF GOD

It is strange to believe that God can stir up disloyalty against people. But the scriptures give us several references of such. Many do not understand that Solomon never had betrayals until he 'messed' with God:

The Cause (The seed)
'And the Lord was angry with Solomon, because his heart was turned from the Lord God of Israel, which had appeared unto him twice.'
1 Kings 11:9.

The Effect (The harvest)
'And the Lord stirred up an adversary unto Solomon, Hadad the Edomite: he was of the king's seed in Edom.' 1 Kings 11:14.

23   And God stirred him up another adversary, Rezon the son of Eliadah, which fled from his lord Hadadezer king of Zobah.

24   And he gathered men unto him, and became captain over a band, when David slew them of Zobah: and they went to Damascus, and dwelt therein, and reigned in Damascus.

25   And he was an adversary to Israel all the days of Solomon, beside the mischief that Hadad did: and he abhorred Israel, and reigned over Syria.

26   And Jeroboam the son of Nebat, an Ephrathite of Zereda, Solomon's servant, whose mother's name was Zeruah, a widow woman, even he lifted up his hand against the king.'
1 Kings 11:23-26.

The bible verses above show the law of cause and effect. Therefore, sometimes; before you scream about betrayal, check yourself to be sure it is not the law of seedtime and harvest (or cause and effect) that is in operation.

The sad part of this is that; though your betraying is an act of God, yet it won't insulate you from the repercussions of being a betrayer.

'The Son of man goeth as it is written of him: but woe unto that man by whom the Son of man is betrayed! It had been good for that man if he had not been born. Mathew 26:24.

'In one sense the Son of Man is entering into a way of treachery well-marked by the Scriptures—no surprises here. In another sense that man who turns him in, turns traitor to the Son of Man—better never to have been born than do this!' The Message.

$$Chapter\ Five$$

DON'T LET BETRAYAL DO THIS TO YOU

WHATEVER YOU COME in contact with has a way of rubbing off on you. Like some specially-concocted perfumes, their fragrance just wouldn't wear off. They last and last and seem to ooze from your very breath. In the same way, having been betrayed, if great care is not taken; betrayal can leave negative indelible marks on your life.

Mimicking the pattern of Paul the Apostle's letters; 'I beseech you therefore brethren, not to allow betrayal do the under-listed to you'.

1.   BREAK CONFIDENCE IN YOURSELF
The key to great accomplishments in life is self confidence. I am excited that it is called "self" confidence because you have the ability to control the confidence. If you don't have confidence in yourself then you shouldn't expect others to.

What betrayal does then is to make you start to doubt yourself. If care is not taken, you start to doubt your ability to make good judgments, discern right and add value. This is why the words of David Levithan, in The Lover's Dictionary ring so true for several people:

"It was a mistake," you said. "But the cruel thing was, it felt like the mistake was mine, for trusting you."
Don't let it break your self confidence.

2.   BREAK CONFIDENCE IN GOD.

For most of us, all we have is God. Don't allow any betrayal to break your confidence in Him. The normal human mind will make you wonder why God allowed it, why He didn't protect you etc. But you need to realize that, although you have lost some things, He is the reason why you have not lost everything.

That is why it is so true that; to refuse to be grateful is to remain a great fool. If you pause to calmly think of the betrayal episode(s), there will always be a reason to praise God. God knows how you feel. He was betrayed by an archangel called Lucifer. Yet He remains God.

After a period of time, you will realize that betrayal is a blessing in disguise. The good thing about all this is that; even if in the heat of the betrayal you have said and done things that are unbecoming of a child of God, all you need to do is repent and rebound. You ought to be glad that even "if we are faithless, He remains faithful, for He cannot deny Himself". 1 Timothy 2:13.

In my hours of trial, my most comforting scripture is Hebrews 13:5-6.
"...for he hath said I will never leave thee, nor forsake thee. So that we may boldly say, The Lord is my helper, and I will not fear what man shall do unto me."
The Amplified Version says:
"..for He [God] Himself has said, I will not in any way fail you nor give you up nor leave you without support. [I will] not, [I will] not,

[I will] not in any degree leave you helpless nor forsake nor let [you] down (relax My hold on you)! [Assuredly not!]"

Little wonder King David (the same person that wrote the lamentation of the betrayed in Psalm 55 eventually) wrote:
"I said to myself, "Relax, the Lord is going to take care of you." Psalms 116:7. New Century Version.
You must keep on saying the same to yourself. And also, remember 'no matter who left you, God will not leave you'. And, as long as God is with you, nothing can shake your root. Remember that 'one with God remains a majority'.

3.   BREAK YOUR TRUST IN HUMANITY
'Sometimes, the person you'd take a bullet for is standing behind the trigger.' Anonymous.

We all need someone. Your purpose cannot be achieved in isolation. In fact any VISION you pursue in ISOLATION will end in DESOLATION. The great industrialist Henry Ford said, "It is better to put four men to work than to do the work of four men".

No matter the level of betrayal you experience, don't let it make you lose trust in humanity. One man's or one group's betrayal does not define all men.
Paul wrote in a letter to the Romans:

'That though betrayal came through one man yet salvation also comes through another man.' Romans 5:17(paraphrased).
 If you shut all men out because one man broke your heart, you would have locked out the man with the healing balm to mend the broken heart.

4.   MAKE YOU BITTER

Don't poison your future with the pain of the past. Stop thinking about the offence; think about God and His power to heal us of our pains, hurts and broken hearts.

'He heals the brokenhearted and binds up their wounds.' Psalms 147:3.

When you think of the offence, the pains and hurts grow, but when you think of God's power they simply go!

What you meditate on grows and what you refuse to give attention simply go. LET IT GO!

Life is all about choices, you can choose to either be bitter or to get better. But please note that bitterness is worse than betrayal because betrayal can only destroy your past but bitterness equally destroys your future.

5.   MAKE YOU REVENGE

Leave the revenge to the expert. His name is God, and you are not God.

Romans 12:19.
'Beloved, do not avenge yourselves, but rather give place to wrath; for it is written, "VENGEANCE IS MINE, I WILL REPAY," says the Lord.'
The Message: 'Don't insist on getting even; that's not for you to do. "I'll do the judging," says God. "I'll take care of it."

As a shepherd and a leader I am aware that all sheep want two things:

1.   Green pastures
2   Still, restful and calm waters

'He maketh me to lie down in green pastures: he leadeth me beside the still waters.' Psalms 23:2.

Ezekiel 34:18 'Some of you eat the greenest grass, then trample down what's left when you finish. Others drink clean water, then step in the water to make the rest of it muddy.
19 All that's left for my flock is what you've trampled down; all they have to drink is water that you've fouled.'

What makes betrayals more painful is what the rascals do in those two verses above. If they can't effect the first one, they ensure they carry out the second part through their words and action. God does not take such lightly. Through His prophet, God has shown us His reaction to such.

God is saying: 'I know you enjoyed the best and got well nurtured from the same church, mentor, leader and organization. However, due to offenses, you are now bastardizing and polluting the mind of others who needs to be nurtured from the same source just like you were'. For such, God will hold them responsible and revenge accordingly. Leave all to God.

Chapter Six

SURVIVAL TOOLS

"The question is never 'will I be betrayed' but 'do I know enough to bounce back from betrayal'? – Anonymous.

The truth is, nobody can teach you how to avoid betrayal, you can only be taught how to survive it. You cannot be more rugged as a leader than Moses, yet he had betrayals from Korah, Dathan and Abiram. (Numbers 16).

I want you to call to heart that Jesus the son of God was betrayed by a member of His inner circle. He was a preacher called Judas from a very prestigious family and reputable tribe. Jesus trusted him so much He put him in charge of the accounts.

I discovered that at most, betrayal is permitted to be a delay, not a denial of success; only a delay, not a defeat. Betrayal comes to all men but the difference is in attitudes. You need not get lost with your losses and you need not break down with your breakdowns. The key thing to always remember is that "Success is the sweetest revenge.' In order for that to happen you have to do these three things:

1.   RELEASE

"It is easier to forgive an enemy than to forgive a friend." William Blake.

You need to make a decision. Decisions create events. You need to make a decision never to allow yourself to be hurt again, which does not mean people will not betray you. They will, but do not allow it to get to you.

Make a decision to always let go and let God. Hurts and pains are unnecessary weights; so drop them and gain speed. Don't poison your future with the pain of the past. Stop complaining, for; the more you complain, the less you obtain. Do not be annoyed, for anger is one letter short of danger.

Release the Prisoner

Release the prisoner. It sounds so casual but it is very deep. This is one of the meanings of the word translated "forgive" in the Bible. Like the parable of the wicked servant whose master released from a debt of $10,000,000, yet he chose to imprison a man that owed him $2,000 (Living Bible Translation of Matthew 18:23-28). We need to release (as from the prison); from our hearts all who offend us, just as God has done for us and is still doing.

Forgiveness is a choice but it's worth it. Unforgiveness is too expensive for us to carry. Someone said "to forgive is to set the prisoner free and discover the prisoner was you". HOW TRUE! You can never know the joy of freedom until you forgive. Little wonder it is said "how much grievous are the consequences of unforgiveness than the cause of it". Learn this great secret, learn to forgive.

2.   RECOVER

"If you're betrayed, release disappointment at once, by that way, the bitterness has no time to take root." - Toba Beta. 'My Ancestor Was an Ancient Astronaut.'

Be quick to recover and bounce back. Many people, when they suffer from betrayal seek to hide it with pretense. My mum taught me that 'the wounds we hide don't heal fast enough'. Maybe we do this to remain popular but popularity is different from happiness. Popularity is when people feel good about you, but happiness is when you feel good about yourself.

Choose to be happy; to be free from guilt. I love this inscription on Dr. John Condor's tomb in Burnhill. "I have trusted, I have loved, I rest, but I shall yet rise again by the grace of God, however unworthy I shall reign." GLORY!
 Make a decision to recover. You might not be able to help where you have been, but you certainly can help where you are going, because I know there are no hopeless situations, only people who think hopelessly.

From my study of papers and people, I know that setbacks should pave way for comebacks; and that 'when the going gets tough, the tough gets going.' "Big shots" I have discovered, are really "small shots" that keep shooting. Please make up your mind never to be moved by situations, rather to move situations.

Now the biggest news of all, you have God! He is greater than the world outside you. 1 John 4:4. I know from experience: "when I am down to nothing my God is up to something!" Therefore, I choose to live my life as an exclamation and not an explanation. It is a choice, a decision.

Now, the next thing to do to fully recover is to move from hindsight to foresight. You have to dream again, for 'your situation is not meant to change your dreams', but rather 'your dreams are to change your situation'. You are not a failure until you allow the regrets of yesterday to take over your dreams of today. Your dreams today are your seeds; you need these seeds to feed later.

Success is not a matter of "luck" but of "pluck". So let go for good whatever does not let you go for God. In your imagination is your manifestation. And let me quickly add 'powerful imagination will produce powerful manifestation'. Les Brown said, "Shoot for the moon, even if your miss it, you will land among the stars." Therefore, he that refuses to think today will surely stink tomorrow. Sit down now and dream again.

Emulate Joseph Jacob (of the Bible). Even if they have taken your coat of many colours, don't let them steal your dream of a great future. You just have to dream better to get better, for it is insight that leads to dispatch in all affairs of life.

Someone said. "If it happens in the mind, it will happen in time". The day to dream again is now! Stop all unnecessary activities; for, 'unnecessary business leads to barrenness'. Your long term dream is your security against short term failures. Dream again...today.

Destiny delayed is the devil's delight. Do it now! Unnecessary idleness paralyses initiative. You need to dream again; for, 'vision is the backbone of distinction'.

## 3.	RESUME

"BETRAYAL must be a COMMA, not a FULL STOP. A delay not a denial. A speed breaker not a destiny stopper."

There is still much to do, so get up, clean up, dress up and show up! Do not build your future around your past, for we serve a God that does not consult our past to determine our future. Thomas Jefferson puts it this way; "I love the dream of the future much more than the history of the past".

Keep-looking forward, not backwards. Take a cue from your physiological make up; God the creator put your eyes in front of your head and not at the back. Why? So that you can be forward-looking and not backward-looking.

One of the incidents in the life of David that made me understand why God called him a man after His own heart is recorded in 2 Samuel 12. When the child born out of his adulterous affair with Bathsheba died, when the child was ill, he (David the King) fasted. He rolled on the ground, without changing his clothes or taking his bath for seven days. He was weeping continuously both night and day. Eventually, the child died but his followers were afraid to tell him fearing that he might die also.

However when David heard them whispering one to another he knew that the child had died. In reacting to this truth, he took a shower, changed his clothes, perfumed and anointed himself. Crazy? So they thought, but unknown to them, David knew one of the greatest secret of all ages, which is:
"Never put a question mark where God has placed a full stop." You can do it too. I know it takes guts to leave the ruts, yet I insist, get moving.

Learn from Jesus, the Master. Hebrews 12:2.
'Looking unto Jesus the author and finisher of our faith; who for the joy that was set before him endured the cross, despising the

shame, and is set down at the right hand of the throne of God.'

It is either you attach yourself to your past or your future. The choice is yours.

Friends, I have been betrayed several times and here are some of the things that helped me:
- I refuse to complain because I know that the more you complain, the less you obtain.
- I refuse to grumble because I know the more you grumble, the more you crumble.

I also refuse to explain the reason for my failure for as a wise man once said: "it takes less time to do something right than it does to explain why you did it wrong." This is why I often say, "some speak from experience, but some from experience don't speak". When I decide to speak, I speak of the good I am expecting, not the 'not so good' that I am experiencing.

I refuse to worry because John Mason said, "worry is a misuse of God's creative imagination which He has placed within us."

In fact, it is discovered that the word "worry" is derived from an Anglo-Saxon word which means to "suffocate".

In any case, my greatest temptation was to fix the blame instead of fixing the problem. When you fix the blame, the problem grows; when you fix the problem, it simply goes. To fix the blame is to get even; to fix the problem is to get ahead.

Chapter Seven

<u>IF YOU ARE THE ONE THAT BETRAYED</u>

WHENEVER I ANNOUNCE the topic of this book, people are always interested. They are quick to point out they have been betrayed before. I find it amusing that hardly do people confess they have betrayed others. Betrayal has two faces!
If many alive have been betrayed, it also means betrayers are equally many; hence the reason for this chapter. It is always great to study men that have walked the ways we are tending to trend and see how they end up.

'Those who betray their own friends leave a legacy of abuse to their children.' Job 17:5.

Paul the Apostle thus admonishes us to:
'Keep in mind those who were over you, and who gave you the word of God; seeing the outcome of their way of life, let your faith be like theirs.' Hebrews 13:7. BBE.

In other words, before you start following them, consider their end.

7 (SEVEN) MAJOR DISLOYAL MEN IN THE BIBLE AND THEIR END

1.   SATAN (THE DEVIL)
Betrayed God his maker

'And the great dragon was cast out, that old serpent, called the Devil, and Satan, which deceiveth the whole world: he was cast out into the earth, and his angels were cast out with him.' Revelation 12:9.

2.   ABSALOM
Betrayed David his father and king

'And ten young men that bare Joab's armour compassed about and smote Absalom, and slew him.' 2 Samuel 18:15.

3.   AHITOPHEL
Betrayed David his Principal and friend

'And when Ahithophel saw that his counsel was not followed, he saddled his ass, and arose, and gat him home to his house, to his city, and put his household in order, and hanged himself, and died, and was buried in the sepulchre of his father.' 2 Samuel 17:23.

4.   SHEMEI
Betrayed David his Principal and friend, ordered to be killed by King Solomon.

'So the king commanded Benaiah the son of Jehoiada; which went out, and fell upon him, that he died. And the kingdom was established in the hand of Solomon.' 1 Kings 2:46.

5.   ADONIJAH
Betrayed King David his father and King Solomon his brother, ordered to be killed by King Solomon.
'And king Solomon sent by the hand of Benaiah the son of Jehoiada; and he fell upon him that he died.' 1 Kings 2:25.

6.   KORAH AND CO
Betrayed Moses, their principal

'And the earth opened her mouth, and swallowed them up, and their houses, and all the men that appertained unto Korah, and all their goods.' Numbers 16:32.
They, and all that appertained to them, went down alive into the pit, and the earth closed upon them: and they perished from among the congregation.' Numbers 16:33.

7.   JUDAS
Betrayed Jesus, his Principal and lord.
'And he cast down the pieces of silver in the temple, and departed, and went and hanged himself.' Mathew 27:5.

THE RETURN OF THE PRODIGAL
11   Then He said: "A certain man had two sons.
12   And the younger of them said to his father, 'Father, give me the portion of goods that falls to me.' So he divided to them his livelihood.
13   And not many days after, the younger son gathered all together, journeyed to a far country, and there wasted his possessions with prodigal living.
14   But when he had spent all, there arose a severe famine in that land, and he began to be in want.

15   Then he went and joined himself to a citizen of that country, and he sent him into his fields to feed swine.

16   And he would gladly have filled his stomach with the pods that the swine ate, and no one gave him anything.

17   But when he came to himself, he said, 'How many of my father's hired servants have bread enough and to spare, and I perish with hunger!

18   I will arise and go to my father, and will say to him, "Father, I have sinned against heaven and before you,

19   And I am no longer worthy to be called your son. Make me like one of your hired servants." '

20   And he arose and came to his father. But when he was still a great way off, his father saw him and had compassion, and ran and fell on his neck and kissed him.

21   And the son said to him, 'Father, I have sinned against heaven and in your sight, and am no longer worthy to be called your son.'

22   But the father said to his servants, 'Bring out the best robe and put it on him, and put a ring on his hand and sandals on his feet.

23   And bring the fatted calf here and kill it, and let us eat and be merry;

24   For this my son was dead and is alive again; he was lost and is found.' And they began to be merry.

25   Now his older son was in the field. And as he came and drew near to the house, he heard music and dancing.

26   So he called one of the servants and asked what these things meant.

27   And he said to him, 'Your brother has come, and because he has received him safe and sound, your father has killed the fatted calf.'

28	But he was angry and would not go in. Therefore his father came out and pleaded with him.
29	So he answered and said to his father, 'Lo, these many years I have been serving you; I never transgressed your commandment at any time; and yet you never gave me a young goat, that I might make merry with my friends.
30	But as soon as this son of yours came, who has devoured your livelihood with harlots, you killed the fatted calf for him.'
31	And he said to him, 'Son, you are always with me, and all that I have is yours.
32	'It was right that we should make merry and be glad, for your brother was dead and is alive again, and was lost and is found.'

Luke 15:11-32.

The book of Luke chapter 15 is exciting on many fronts. It talks about the lost sheep, the lost coin and the lost son (commonly called the prodigal son).

One thing I want you to note is that, out of the three; it was only the prodigal son that came back on his own volition. There is also another deep lesson to be learnt. After the prodigal son betrayed his father and squandered his heritage, he started being in want. '... and he began to be in want.' Luke 15:14.

The 'wants' are mostly multidimensional as expatiated below. Many people who betrayed others will eventually experience one or more of these.

1.   Want of provision

'But when he had spent all, there arose a severe famine in that land, and he began to be in want. Luke 15:14.

It is sad to note that betrayers often end up in want. Initially, they seem to enter into wealth, however; they eventually end up 'to be in want.' They will soon realize that 'real wealth is really in their network and not in the net worth. Furthermore, they will grasp the truth that 'once you betray the source, the sustenance ceases'.

2.   Want of vital relationships

'Then he went and joined himself to a citizen of that country...' Luke 15:15.

Of all the 'ships' to take in order to achieve one's purpose, relation'ships' are the most vital. Sadly enough, traitors discover too late that the folks who fueled the betrayal leave the moment sustenance ceases. That is not surprising though, in the first instance, they came because of what they can gain. Most betrayers soon realize they have to join themselves to "citizens of a strange country, doctrine and ideology."

3.   Want of position and inheritance

18 'I will arise and go to my father, and will say to him, "Father, I have sinned against heaven and before you.
19 And I am no longer worthy to be called your son. Make me like one of your hired servants.'
Luke 15:18-19.

Interestingly, all betrayal starts with unbecoming thoughts. A good example is that, they start feeling they are better off separated than cooperating within that body they belong to. To their amazement, they soon realize that 'most times it is better to be the leg of an elephant than be the head of an ant.' (Selah). The realization of 'I am no longer worthy' is a dangerous position to be in.

I normally tell my biological children that they should observe I sometimes send them on the same errands I send the maids, whereas I pay the maids salary while they don't get paid. The difference is that, the reward of the maids is in their income but theirs is in their inheritance.

It is a terrible thing to forfeit eventual inheritance because of instant income. (In the bible, Esau gave us a good illustration of this truth).

Retracing your steps from betrayal
Taking a cue from the prodigal son, those who betray can always retrace their steps by doing the following:

1.   REALIZE
Betrayal does that ... betrays the betrayer. Erica Jong - Becoming Light.

The greatest meeting in life is the one with yourself.
'But when he came to himself...' Luke 15:17.

The prodigal son earlier met with his dad and got resources but not sustenance. He met with his employer and got 'meager income' instead of 'mega inheritance', until he finally set up a meeting with himself!

To retrace your steps, you have to shut out all meetings with others and schedule a meeting with you. Such meetings help you to realize that you have made a huge mistake and start a journey of retracing your steps.

## 2.	REPENT

"When you betray somebody else, you also betray yourself." Isaac Bashevis Singer.

Repent. What a powerful word. It means to change course of direction after realizing and renouncing your betrayal.

The steps to repentance is to regret, renounce then repent. Each of these steps is essential. To truly repent, you have to regret then renounce.

We can see these steps clearly with the prodigal son. He followed through each of these.

Regret
'But when he came to himself, he said, 'How many of my father's hired servants have bread enough and to spare, and I perish with hunger!' Luke 15:17.

Renounce
'And I am no longer worthy to be called your son. Make me like one of your hired servants.' Luke 15:19.

Repent
'I will arise and go to my father, and will say to him, "Father, I have sinned against heaven and before you.' Luke 15:18.

3.   RETURN

"Sometimes the best way forward is backwards."

Returning is the final icing on the cake in retracing your steps. All other steps would have been futile if the prodigal son did not do this.

'And he arose and came to his father...' Luke 15:20.

It takes action to birth restoration. Stand up now, since you have realized and repent. You must thus complete the circle and return. Do not return with the attitude of entitlement to restoration but with an attitude of repentance. The boy in Luke 15 said

'I don't necessarily want to be returned into my position but I just want to be in your good disposition.'

WARNING TO THE FATHERS

Someone told me that for him the number 3 had been very difficult. He, like the prodigal had realized, repented but has tried to return but the father refused to even see him. This is an admonition to all fathers to emulate God. We must be willing to warmly embrace and receive the return of the prodigals.

You don't necessarily need to place them back in their position in the organization, but bless them with your good disposition. In addition, help them with a fresh start on their own or somewhere else (if not in your own organization).

WARNING TO THE ELDER BROTHERS

 29 'So he answered and said to his father, 'Lo, these many years I have been serving you; I never transgressed your commandment at any time; and yet you never gave me a young goat, that I might make merry with my friends.

30 But as soon as this son of yours came, who has devoured your livelihood with harlots, you killed the fatted calf for him.
31 And he said to him, 'Son, you are always with me, and all that I have is yours.
32 It was right that we should make merry and be glad, for your brother was dead and is alive again, and was lost and is found.'
Luke 15:29-32

Dear 'elder brother', I understand your feelings and disposition. You stayed, you suffered until the organization survived and thrived again and now the prodigal is back to the father's warm embrace.

The elder brothers are those who stayed back in the father's presence. They are those who loyally served the father without asking for reward. When the 'younger brother' who has lavished the father's inheritance came back into music and party, they are always sad. That is quite understandable. They kept labouring while the waster left the house.

I am aware that the love of the father is always greater than the love of the brother. I am also aware that the reward of them that stayed is always greater than the reward of them that strayed! Remain immovable!

EPILOGUE
MOVE ON WITH COURAGE - VICTORY IS SURE

'He who loses wealth loses much, he who loses a friend loses more, but he who loses courage loses all, since one man with God is still a majority.' Miguel Cevantes.

An old sage said: "With optimism, I anticipate a virile, buoyant tomorrow even from generations yet unborn, if only we do not succumb to the pressure of today."

You have to work out your dream, for what you don't work out will never show out; and the way to the top is to get off the bottom.

For 'until you are ready to work, nothing works'. You cannot just sit down and wish for a change, it does not come by wishing, but by pushing.

Thomas Edison the great scientist said, 'Success is 99% perspiration and 1% inspiration." Somebody said, "Actions may not always bring happiness, but there can never be happiness without an action."
Nobody gets ahead without first sticking out his neck; even a turtle is wise enough to know this.

Note that; there are a lot of ways to become a failure, but never taking a chance is the surest and most effective. You have to take chances, so you need the courage that only Christ gives.

For, 'it takes both a dreaming mind and a working hand to produce a winning man'. Yes! Success is usually a partnership between the "brains" and the "biceps".

Don't bother waiting for someone to come and help you or you'll have to wait for long. Really, the best helping hands you will ever get are the ones attached to your shoulder blades. It does not matter where you are today, everyone that got where they are started from where they were. Somebody said. "The secret of success is to start from the scratch and keep scratching".

Remember that 'God created the world out of nothing'. Even if you think there is nothing; God is an expert in creating something out of nothing (Hebrews 11:1-3). Until you release your potentials, destiny cannot be released. Try and try hard, for even "triumph" is just "UMPH" added to "Try" Dare to dream again!

If you do as it is written in this book, then victory is sure, but the decision is not a product of resolutions but of revelations. You know that resolutions never last, what you actually need is a revelation in Christ. It is decision based on a discovery.

The Bible says, "Whosoever decides for Him shall be saved." Somebody said, "I remain neutral." No! That is impossible. 'Not deciding to succeed is deciding to fail'. So not deciding for Christ is deciding against Him, and it is either Christ or crisis, the choice is yours.

DO IT NOW, it is as simple as ABC.

A.   Accept your need for a Savior.
B.   Believe Jesus is the Son of God and the savior of the world.
C.   Confess that with your mouth (Romans 10:9-15). You are SAVED.

SEE YOU AT THE TOP!

Author's Profile

ALBERT OLUFEMI ODUWOLE oversees many organizations worldwide including the TRIUMPHANT NATION; a fast growing network of churches.

He is the CEO of "Get Inspired Inc." a peak performance Consulting Incorporation. He is well sought after by several civic, corporate and Christian organizations to train in Africa, Asia, Europe and North America.

He is an international certified relationship coach with over 25 years' experience and holds online and onsite LOVE CLINICS that attracts thousands of people across nations, congregations and generations.

He has been happily married to his lovely wife TJ for over two decades and together they preside over WORD ABLAZE MISSION INTERNATIONAL - a multifaceted mission comprising an international outreach ministry, training centres, publishing outfit, media corporation and a fast-growing network of churches, TRIUMPHANT NATION EVERYWHERE.

OTHER BOOKS BY THE SAME AUTHOR

GET INSPIRED SERIES
 GET INSPIRED MOTIVATION
 GET INSPIRED RELATIONSHIP
 31 DAYS MAKEOVER : GET INSPIRED EVERYDAY

EXPLOITS OF FAITH SERIES
 DYNAMICS OF BREAKTHROUGH
 INVEST OR DIFUSE
 UNLOCKING POWER FOR EXPLOITS
 DARE TO DREAM AGAIN
 BREAKING FORTH INTO DESTINY

OTHERS

I STILL DO
I LOVE MY SPOUSE BUT
RUNNING WITH A VISION
THE PROSTITUES APPROACH TO BUSINESS
The exploits of faith
7 things champions do before breakfast
MARRYmatics : The formulae for marrying right

www.ingramcontent.com/pod-product-compliance
Lightning Source LLC
Chambersburg PA
CBHW020935160726
47993CB00007B/2793